FLOOD WARNING

BY KATHARINE KENAH

ILLUSTRATED BY AMY SCHIMLER-SAFFORD

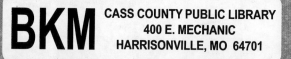
HARPER
An Imprint of HarperCollinsPublishers

Special thanks to Dr. Christopher Kenah, Geologist, Division of Drinking and Ground Waters, Ohio Environmental Protection Agency, for his valuable assistance.

The Let's-Read-and-Find-Out Science book series was originated by Dr. Franklyn M. Branley, Astronomer Emeritus and former Chairman of the American Museum–Hayden Planetarium, and was formerly co-edited by him and Dr. Roma Gans, Professor Emeritus of Childhood Education, Teachers College, Columbia University. Text and illustrations for each of the books in the series are checked for accuracy by an expert in the relevant field. For more information about Let's-Read-and-Find-Out Science books, write to HarperCollins Children's Books, 195 Broadway, New York, NY 10007, or visit our website at www.letsreadandfindout.com.

Library of Congress Control Number: 2016936036
ISBN 978-0-06-238662-5 (trade bdg.) — ISBN 978-0-06-238661-8 (pbk.)

The artist used mixed media collage to create the digital illustrations for this book.
Typography by Erica De Chavez
16 17 18 19 20   SCP   10 9 8 7 6 5 4 3 2 1
❖
First Edition

For my constantly curious family, with love—K.K.
For Charlie and his growing umbrella collection—A.S.

You are lying in bed listening to the soft sound of rain. It has been coming down for hours.

Now something is changing. The rain sounds harder and louder. Tiny streaks of raindrops on your window have turned into sheets of water. There is so much water running down the roads, they look like small rivers. Puddles have turned into lakes.

What is happening?
You are hearing and seeing the start of a flood.

We couldn't live without water, but water on the move can be dangerous. Too much water in the wrong place is a **flood**.

Rain comes down all over the world. It rains on mountains and fields. It rains on cities and towns. It rains on people, plants, and pets. No matter where the rain comes down, it finds its way into rivers. Rivers carry rainwater back to the sea.

Don't Go Swimming Here!

Cherrapunji, India, is one of the wettest places on earth. It averages 463 inches of rain a year!

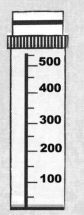

The Atacama Desert in South America is one of the driest places on earth. It averages less than an inch of rain a year.

A flood happens when land that is usually dry is covered with water. It may happen slowly, over hours and days, or it may happen in minutes. It may start nearby, or hundreds of miles away. Floods come in all different sizes and start for different reasons.

One flood might leave an inch of water in a basement.

Another flood might move the house.
Some are so big, they wash away towns.

The ground is like a sponge. It will soak up water for a while, but when it is full of water, it can't soak up any more. The ground becomes **saturated**.

Runoff, water that can't sink into the ground, will flow toward the lowest places around.

Trees make the ground more like a sponge. Rainwater flows down holes and tunnels made by their roots.

Floodwater doesn't flow in a straight line. It moves sideways, up and down, and swirls around. That **turbulent** motion gives floodwater the power to pick up small rocks, dirt, sand, and debris and transport it somewhere else. When the floodwater slows down, it drops the materials it has carried.

Most floods are **river floods**. They begin when heavy rainstorms or melting ice and snow pour more water into streams than they usually carry. Small streams become big streams. Together they pour huge amounts of extra water into rivers.

Rivers get so full of water that they spill over their banks onto low, flat land. The land that gets flooded beside a river is the river's **floodplain**.

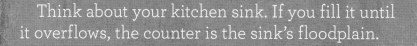

Think about your kitchen sink. If you fill it until it overflows, the counter is the sink's floodplain.

Most river floods build slowly, but **flash floods** are much more dangerous. They happen *so* fast, no one knows they are coming!

Flash floods start when heavy rainstorms move slowly over mountains. So much rainwater pours down, it can't all soak into the ground. Runoff water flows down mountain slopes into the narrow river valleys and rocky canyons below. The water level in a river gets higher and higher, and it turns into a raging flood racing downstream.

Flash floods can also happen in cities. Water can't soak through roads, sidewalks, or buildings, so it runs along streets, pours through sewer drains, and floods subway tunnels.

There is no way to stop a flash flood, or outrun it. The safest thing to do is to move to higher ground.

19

Imagine that you live in a house on a beach. The view out your window is beautiful—waves rolling in and out, sand castles and seashells dotting the sand, families having picnics.

But now the sun disappears behind large, dark clouds. Waves are getting higher and rougher. No one is on the beach.

What is happening?

You are about to be hit by a hurricane, and maybe a **coastal flood**!

Most coastal floods are caused by hurricanes,
storms so big they can be seen by satellites.
Hurricanes move over the ocean like whirling
doughnuts of wind and rain. When a hurricane
gets close to land, its powerful winds make
the ocean waves go wild and they get higher
and stronger.

A massive amount of seawater called a **storm surge** is driven onshore by the wind and waves. The water keeps pouring onto land until the storm has passed, and can sometimes reach twenty feet above sea level.

The storm surge and waves roar into coastal cities and towns, flooding everything in their path. It can take months, even years, to repair all the damage.

Coastal floods can also happen for another reason: **tsunamis**! The seafloor isn't flat and still like the bottom of a bathtub. There are erupting volcanoes, earthquakes, and landslides on the ocean floor. The outward force of these events moves unseen through the ocean until it rises up as a *giant* wall of water when it reaches land.

People don't always know a tsunami is coming, but some animals can tell. In 2004, Sri Lanka was hit by one of the biggest tsunamis ever recorded.

Before it arrived, elephants began stamping on the ground and running to higher ground. They could feel small vibrations in the earth through their feet.

Never think floodwater can't hurt you. Even though a flooded area may look shallow, the water may be deeper than it looks and there could be dangerous debris underneath.

Floodwater is dirty and heavy. Six inches of rapidly moving water can knock you down. Two feet of rapidly moving water can float a bus and sweep away cars.

If you are approaching floodwaters while you are walking, driving, or biking, you'll stay safe if you remember this rule: *Turn around; don't drown.*

To prepare for a flood, make a **flood plan** with your family. Know what safety supplies you'll need, and pick a safe meeting place that is on high ground or in a tall, strong building where you can meet in case you are separated during a flood.

1. Water – 3-day supply
   1 gallon per person

2. Food – 3-day supply

3. Flashlight and batteries

4. Battery-powered radio

5. First-aid kit

6. Emergency blanket

7. Rain gear

8. Multipurpose tools

9. Pet supplies

Floods are not all bad. In many parts of the world, they are expected and welcomed as part of the natural cycle. For thousands of years, farmers have relied on annual floods to bring freshwater to their crops and new **sediment** to their land. Sediment is made of very fine grains of sand, silt, and clay, and it puts nutrients back into fields. Sediment works like a vitamin pill for crops!

Ancient Egyptians celebrated the beginning of the River Nile's annual flood. That was the start of their new year.

But with no control, floodwaters can spill over river valleys, drowning crops and washing away seeds and soil.

What can control a flood? A **dam**. Dams are walls built across rivers to hold back water and regulate how much goes through. The water that collects behind a dam forms a lake called a **reservoir**. Many towns and cities get their water from reservoirs.

Levees are earthen or concrete walls built on floodplains to protect cities, towns, and farms from river floods.

People are not the only ones who build dams. Beavers use sticks and mud to build dams across creeks. The water that backs up behind their dams gives them a safe place to build their homes.

Meteorologists are scientists who study weather. They use information from satellites and radar to study weather conditions over a wide area. If a flood is possible, they issue a **flood watch** so people have time to prepare and to stock up on bottled water, batteries for flashlights and radios, canned food, and first-aid supplies.

If communities close to water are in danger, people fill bags with sand and build **sandbag walls** around their homes to keep water out.

If a **flood warning** is issued, a flood is on its way. It's not time to be afraid. It's time to take action! If the flood is a big one, experts may decide it's best to leave the area, so you may be told to **evacuate** your home.

33

Floods are powerful. If one is on its way, you know what to do to stay safe. Gather the supplies you'll need, move to a high place, and pay close attention to any flood warning!

Glossary

Coastal flood—When seawater floods onto the normally dry land along a coast.

Dam—A wall built across a river to control the flow of water.

Evacuate—To leave a dangerous place, such as your home, if a dangerous flood is coming.

Flash flood—A dangerous flood that happens very quickly.

Flood—A rising and overflowing of water onto land that is usually dry.

Floodplain—The low land that gets flooded beside a river.

Flood plan—A list of what to take with you and where to meet in a flood emergency.

Flood warning—An official announcement that a flood is coming.

Flood watch—An official announcement that a flood is possible.

Levees—Earthen walls built on floodplains to restrict a flooded area.

Meteorologist—A scientist who studies weather.

Reservoir—A lake that forms behind a dam.

River flood—A flood that occurs when an unusually full river spills water onto low land.

Runoff—Water that can't soak into saturated ground.

Sandbag wall—A wall built with sandbags around homes and buildings to protect them from floods.

Saturated—When the ground is too full to absorb more water.

Sediment—Fine grains of sand, silt, and clay picked up by rivers.

Storm surge—A wall of water pushed onto land by hurricane winds.

Tsunami—A giant ocean wave, usually set off by an undersea earthquake or a volcanic eruption.

Turbulent—The active motion that gives floodwater the power to transport materials.

Find Out More
Super Sponge!

The ground is like a sponge, and when it is saturated, it can't take in any more water. If floodwater can't soak into the ground, it keeps on moving. In this activity, your sponge will act like the ground. See what happens when you cause a flood!

Materials:
- Clean, dry sponge
- Pan or cookie sheet with sides (on flat surface)

Put a sponge in the middle of a pan or cookie sheet and pour water slowly onto the sponge. Make sure you pour it evenly over the sponge, not just in one spot. See what happens as you pour. When the water begins to seep out around the bottom of the sponge, it is becoming saturated. Keep pouring and see it become even more saturated! Water flows over the whole surface of the sponge because it can't absorb any more.

Tip up the pan, with the saturated sponge at the top. What happens? Imagine the pan is the side of a mountain. Can you see why a narrow river valley at the base of mountains might be in trouble after a heavy rainstorm?

Transport Power!

Floodwater doesn't flow along smoothly. It moves up and down and swirls around. It is active! That active motion gives floods the power to transport materials from one place to another. When the floodwater slows down, it drops the materials it has created. In this experiment, you'll create transport power inside a jar!

Materials:
- Clear glass jar with a lid
- Materials to be tested, such as marbles, sand, dirt, rice, paper clips, toothpicks, or marshmallows!

Put a small amount of each of the materials in the jar. Fill the jar with water almost to the top, put the lid on tightly, then shake it! Swirl the jar up, down, and all around until the material in the jar is thoroughly mixed with the water. Set it on a flat surface and watch what happens. What floats the longest? Which drops out first? What would happen if the materials were being transported in a real flood?

To find out more about floods, you can visit the following websites:

What to Do Before, During, and After a Flood
www.ready.gov/kids/know-the-facts/floods

Facts about Floods
www.fema.gov/media-library/assets/documents/34288

To see video of extreme flooding in Yosemite National Park, visit www.nps.gov/yose/learn/photosmultimedia/yosemitepresents.htm

Be sure to look for all of these books in the Let's-Read-and-Find-Out Science series:

 LEVEL 1

The Human Body:
How Many Teeth?
I'm Growing!
My Feet
My Five Senses
My Hands
Sleep Is for Everyone
What's for Lunch?

Plants and Animals:
Animals in Winter
Baby Whales Drink Milk
Big Tracks, Little Tracks
Bugs Are Insects
Dinosaurs Big and Small
Ducks Don't Get Wet
Fireflies in the Night
From Caterpillar to Butterfly
From Seed to Pumpkin
From Tadpole to Frog
How Animal Babies Stay Safe
How a Seed Grows
A Nest Full of Eggs
Starfish
A Tree Is a Plant
What Lives in a Shell?
What's Alive?
What's It Like to Be a Fish?
Where Are the Night Animals?
Where Do Chicks Come From?

The World Around Us:
Air Is All Around You
The Big Dipper
Clouds
Is There Life in Outer Space?
Pop!
Snow Is Falling
Sounds All Around
The Sun and the Moon
What Makes a Shadow?

LEVEL 2

The Human Body:
A Drop of Blood
Germs Make Me Sick!
Hear Your Heart
The Skeleton Inside You
What Happens to a Hamburger?
Why I Sneeze, Shiver, Hiccup, and Yawn
Your Skin and Mine

Plants and Animals:
Almost Gone
Ant Cities
Be a Friend to Trees
Chirping Crickets
Corn Is Maize
Dolphin Talk
Honey in a Hive
How Do Apples Grow?
How Do Birds Find Their Way?
Life in a Coral Reef
Look Out for Turtles!
Milk from Cow to Carton
An Octopus Is Amazing
Penguin Chick
Sharks Have Six Senses
Snakes Are Hunters
Spinning Spiders
Sponges Are Skeletons
What Color Is Camouflage?
Who Eats What?
Who Lives in an Alligator Hole?
Why Do Leaves Change Color?
Why Frogs Are Wet
Wiggling Worms at Work
Zipping, Zapping, Zooming Bats

Dinosaurs:
Did Dinosaurs Have Feathers?
Digging Up Dinosaurs
Dinosaur Bones
Dinosaur Tracks
Dinosaurs Are Different
Fossils Tell of Long Ago
My Visit to the Dinosaurs
What Happened to the Dinosaurs?
Where Did Dinosaurs Come From?

Space:
Floating in Space
The International Space Station
Mission to Mars
The Moon Seems to Change
The Planets in Our Solar System
The Sky Is Full of Stars
The Sun
What Makes Day and Night
What the Moon Is Like

Weather and the Seasons:
Down Comes the Rain
Feel the Wind
Flash, Crash, Rumble, and Roll
Hurricane Watch
Sunshine Makes the Seasons
Tornado Alert
What Will the Weather Be?

Our Earth:
Archaeologists Dig for Clues
Earthquakes
Flood Warning
Follow the Water from Brook to Ocean
How Deep Is the Ocean?
How Mountains Are Made
In the Rainforest
Let's Go Rock Collecting
Oil Spill!
Volcanoes
What Happens to Our Trash?
What's So Bad About Gasoline?
Where Do Polar Bears Live?
Why Are the Ice Caps Melting?
You're Aboard Spaceship Earth

The World Around Us:
Day Light, Night Light
Energy Makes Things Happen
Forces Make Things Move
Gravity Is a Mystery
How People Learned to Fly
Light Is All Around Us
Simple Machines
Switch On, Switch Off
What Is the World Made Of?
What Makes a Magnet?
Where Does the Garbage Go?